Spark a Story
101 Writing Prompts
to Kindle the Imagination

I0101577

Written and Illustrated
by Debby Johnson

Loveblind Publishing
P.O. Box 8236
Moreno Valley, CA 92552
www.loveblindpublishing.com

Ordering Information:
Quantity sales. Special discounts are available on quantity purchases by corporations, associations, and others. For details, contact the publisher at the address above.

Orders by U.S. trade bookstores and wholesalers. For details, contact the publisher at the address above.

ISBN-10: 0692675736

ISBN-13: 978-0692675731 (LoveBlind Publishing)

DEDICATION

To writers everywhere. Yes, that means you!

Here you'll find inspiration bound in the pages of a book, scattered with truths and frivolity.

Let your mind wander and your words flow.

CONTENTS

ACKNOWLEDGMENTS

Many thanks to Ron and Christopher Johnson, my chief proofreaders and tireless cheerleaders.

This would not have been possible without you.

I would also be remiss if I didn't acknowledge my writing students who regularly keep me on my toes as well as faithfully doing their writing exercises to help build up their creative muscles, one word at a time.

WHAT'S THE POINT?

You want to write more than anything else in the world but you're afraid to start, or you don't know where to start. Struggling to find both the time and inspiration makes it even harder to become a writer.

There you are, trying to move towards your lifelong dream of being a writer, and something always seems to hold you back It might be your crazy little inner voice that tells you that you can't do it , or some one else who asks the question "You really think you're a writer?"

You can only suck in air, standing there as they puncture your confidence, and deflate your dream with six little words. Oh yeah, most of them will then be happy to ask the next question, too. "How many people actually get published?"

Let me give you some help with a response. Will you ever get published if you don't write? Ummm...no.

So, what's the point? The point is that writers write. They don't think about writing or talk about writing. They write. They write because they have no other choice than to spill the words out upon the page.

When you don't know what to write you use some tools. Like writing prompts. Even if you do know what you want to write, if you're stumbling around, trying to find the right scene or the best story arc, grabbing a writing prompt and warming up can help.

Yes. **Warm up**. Writing prompts are for writers what stretches are for athletes. I bet you never thought about it that way, did you? I teach karate classes — believe me I don't want my students jumping out on the floor and doing a roundhouse kick without a little warm up. No way! So prime the writing pump with these 101 prompts. You never know, you just might find the seed of a story idea that grows and blossoms into a full-fledged novel.

Don't believe its possible? I do. I'm working on a novel that sprouted from the tiny seed of an idea — a writing a prompt.

Sit down. Write. That's the simple recipe for writing success.

You can do it. ***Start now.***

LET THE FUN BEGIN -

1. A boulder came crashing down from the mountain headed directly at our car and...

2. The old man turned the brittle key in the lock...

3. A vibrant butterfly with huge fangs landed on my neck and...

4. A huge rumble vibrated the ground just before....

5. Santa slid down the chimney and landed...

> **The glimmer of an idea can turn into an entire story, if you just let your mind go and embrace the possibilities.**

6. The life of a peanut butter sandwich

7. A snake slithered out from under the couch…

8. All I could see was the smothering darkness in the cave until….

9. If a paintbrush could talk, what would it say?

10. I bit into an apple and felt…

Ideas can come from anywhere and everywhere. Once your creativity has been sparked you just might be inundated with story ideas. Find a system to keep track of them so that you can continue writing your WIP (work in progress).

11. The cat nimbly jumped up to the keyboard and began to type...

12. Just as I went to swat the mosquito buzzing at my ear, I heard...

13. My dog barked in Morse code, saying...

14. The old lady rocked in her chair chanting...

15. There was a handwritten note on my doorstep. It said...

16. I hiccupped and time literally stood still…

17. A butterfly flitted by, pulling a banner that read…

18. An officer pulled me over and said…

19. Just as the baby screamed…

20. On the shelf, in the old cabin, I found a jar full of…

21. The eagle soared down, and used its massive talons to snatch up...

22. You're a popsicle melting on a countertop.

23. The sun burned through the clouds, illuminating...

24. In the sky, a helicopter flew upside down...

25. Groggy, she lifted the cup to her lips, but instead of coffee she tasted...

26. Waves threatened to capsize the ship as the captain ordered...

27. A hamburger and fries have a conversation.

{ JUST WRITE.

EDIT LATER. }

28. The car slowly drove down the deserted street. As it rounded the corner...

29. The life of a post-it.

30. A teacher suddenly finds herself a student, in her own class.

31. She thrust her hand into the dark hole and felt....

32. A howl filled the night just as the moon dipped behind the clouds. That's when...

33. The shovel bit into metal. That's when he...

34. The casket lid slowly opened and...

35. The spider wove a web around...

Go with the first thing that pops into your head. Drop the words on the page.

Just write.

36. An old woman touched the child and it...

37. The baby's scream pierced the silence just as...

38. A grasshopper dove into a bowl of soup and...

39. A conversation between a piece of paper and a pencil.

40. The leaves rustled in the wind. She could hear them saying...

41. Tiny droplets of water splashed down hitting him as...

42. An empty bottle marked the spot where ...

43. A scarecrow engages a bird in a conversation.

44. After the end of the battle, only two soldiers remained standing. They...

45. The canoe shot over the rapids. They never saw....

Edit.

Don't let it become a
four-letter word.
Embrace the process.

46. The drycleaner pulled the hanger from the rack.
    On it was…

47. She cried huge tears when she saw the stranger…

48. An open book lay on the bench. The first sentence
    read…

49. He hiccupped as he fell and…

50. She answered the phone and a
    raspy voice said…

51. What would a
    light bulb say if
    it could talk?

52. She glanced at
    her reflection
    in the mirror.
    But it wasn't there.

53. He sliced through the taut rope and heard the
    sound of something falling.

54. You're an apple in a child's lunch box.

55. They were tied to a tree when the fire started.

56. An atomic bomb exploded. There are only two people left. You and who else?

57. The old woman slipped on the ice, shattering...

58. Two ants vie to see who is the strongest.

59. She slipped him a note that said....

60. He found an old brown wallet on the street. When he opened it he found...

61. She could hear a voice. But no one was there.

62. The judge leaned down to the defendant and said…

63. The last words of a condemned man.

64. A squirrel found itself in the lion's cage at the zoo.

65. A teenager spilled paint all over the new carpet

SILENCE YOUR INNER CRITIC.

GIVE IT A NAME AND THEN TELL IT TO SHUT UP.

WRITE A STORY WHERE HE OR SHE GOES AWAY AND NEVER COMES BACK.

Write at least three pages every day.
Write ten minutes every day.
Make your writing important.
WRITE.

66. He looked at his freshly inked tattoo and spoke.

67. The power lines overhead drooped dangerously low to the ground as…

68. A coffee bean that's been spilled into a grinder.

69. The phone rang. She glanced at the name on the caller ID and…

70. A cat stuck up on the roof of a house, trying to get down.

71. A weed sprouted in the middle of a flowerbed and said...

72. A lizard trying to cross the road.

73. He looked at the old black and white photo recognizing...

74. The light turned green and the driver didn't budge, so...

75. The student crumpled up his test, tossing it to the trash as...

76. The explorer stepped into the swamp and…

77. A giant snake drops down from a tree and lands on you.

78. Two rollie pollies having a conversation.

79. A rocket lands on Jupiter and discovers…

80. He received a mysterious text message. It said…

THE THREE-STEP PROCESS
TO BECOME A WRITER.
GUARANTEED TO WORK.

1. Sit down.

2. Write.

3. Write some more.

A writer writes. If you're not putting down your own unique thoughts and ideas then you're not a writer. So, sit down, and start writing. Simple, huh?

81. You abducted an alien.

82. A stranger drops a letter into your mailbox. It says...

83. You're listening to two babies babble and suddenly realize that you can understand what they're saying.

84. There's a knock at your front door. The FBI is standing there...

85. You find a bottle washed up on the shore. Inside it is...

86. He dove into the pool and discovered…

87. She opened the front door and found a package on the doorstep. Ripping it open she found…

88. A mysterious email arrives in your inbox. It promises….

89. You answer the phone to hear a deep gravelly voice saying, "You're going to die within 24 hours."

90. You see someone dressed exactly like you. Then you realize you're looking at yourself.

91. You're floating in the ocean.

92. A spaceship lands in your backyard.

93. Tiny ants carry off your cell phone.

94. In the back of the cupboard you find an old pink jar. You open it and...

95. A seagull swoops down and steals....

96. All of the doors in your house slam shut at the same instant.

97. Clocks worldwide refuse to move forward in time. They are still running but time is standing still.

98. Someone whispers your name. You turn around. No one is there.

99. The calendar says July 24th but it's snowing outside.

100. You're stranded in the desert with only a paperclip, one bottle of water and a book.

101. Your puppy rushes to the door when you get home. Only, instead of barking hello, he says....

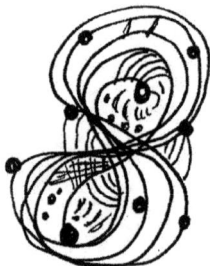

MY MUSINGS

Did you see the writing on the cover of the book and wonder what it said? It's not just there to look pretty, it's also a message to you— the reader. Kind of a cheerleading, put your butt in the chair, and write kind of message.

Since you can't read it too well on the cover, I thought I'd help you out and include it inside. Here goes — the musings from inside my head.

Writer's block and procrastination have killed many great stories. Couple that with the dreaded inner critic and it is amazing that any stories are ever written.

Break through the block and find inspiration all around you. Use this book to help you generate new story ideas and to provide you plenty of opportunities to write. Let's face it, all great athletes practice and practice to get good at their sports, right? And a painter doesn't grab a paintbrush and instantly produce a masterpiece. *It takes practice.* You could use these prompts and practice every single day for one hundred and one days. Think about that. The ***power of practice*** added to the new ideas flooding your brain ***could* turn you from a person who talks about writing in to a person who actually writes.** You know, a writer!

Imagine that. Let these little blips of ideas help to take you along the path toward achieving your lifetime goal. **One little prompt at a time. One little word at a time.** The first step is always the most important. Until you take that step and begin the journey on the path you'll never be a writer.

So, what's stopping you? Nothing but yourself. Believe in the power of you. You can do anything that you want to do. Honest. I wouldn't lie.

So, why aren't you writing yet? Are you waiting until you have the best idea of all time? That's a silly excuse. Start practicing today. Are you waiting to get a special pen or an expensive pad of paper? Ha. Those are just excuses. Some great words have been penned on napkins and matchbook covers. Your next excuse? It's getting tougher and tougher to come up with one, isn't it? Yeah, that's what I thought. Come on, crack the cover of this book and start with writing prompt number one.

You can do it. I have faith in you. I believe in you. Grab a pen, read the prompt and just put the very first thing that pops into your brain down on paper.

It doesn't even have to be good. It just has to be written. You can clean it all up and make it brilliant once you spill those initial thoughts down on paper. See! *One prompt a day and you'll be a writer.*

ABOUT THE AUTHOR

Quirky and unpredictable are just a couple of words that could describe Debby Johnson. She's also passionate about lists. Yes...a diehard list maker, she believes that one day she'll actually accomplish all of the items that she's set out to complete.

As of now her completed list looks like this:

1. Business owner of a graphic design firm where she serves as the owner/creative director/general flunky

2. Karate instructor and second degree black belt in Shotokan karate. She aspires to be the oldest practitioner of this art one day and finds it incredibly cool that she shares her birthday with Sensei Funakoshi, the founder of Shotokan karate.

3. She teaches creative writing classes as well as works as a writing coach. She loves hearing her students stories.

4. She's a painter and mixed media artist, having shown her work in various galleries, including one in Switzerland.

5. Most importantly she is married to a very talented singer/songwriter/musician, Ron, and has five great kids. Rounding out the family are adorable puppies Pixel, Coco and Sadie along with Zanshin the turtle and Macaroni, the cat. Her happy menagerie lives in Southern California.

OTHER BOOKS BY DEBBY JOHNSON

Books include:

Poetry
- Suburbia and other signposts pointing west

Illustrated books for children
- Rock Paper Scissors
- Brainiac Zac and the Mischievous Letters

Contributor to:
- Cookie: A Love Story
- Chicken Soup for the Soul:
  My Very Good, Very Bad Dog
- Chicken Soup for the Soul: The Joy of Less

Coming Soon:

- Penelope Anne Curse of the Mermaid's Treasure
  (chapter book for children)

- The Great Fourth Grade Marshmallow Wars
  (chapter book for children)

CAPTURE THEM

Create your own writing prompts. Jot down your story ideas. Sketch out a character profile. Use this space to write something that motivates you. Or something that inspires you. Plop down anything — make it something that makes you write more.

Ready...set...go!

_____

_____

_____

_____

_____

_____

_____

_____

_____

_____

_____

_____

_____

_____

_____

_____

_____

CREATIVITY & DOODLING

You don't have to believe me, but it's true. Doodling is a great trigger for creativity. When you allow your brain to relax and engage visually, something wonderful happens. You spark creativity.

Remember back to when you were in school, or sitting in a recent business meeting. Your mind wandered and you absent-mindedly picked up a pen or pencil, letting it doodle across your paper. A torrent of ideas flooded into your brain.

Try it now. Relax. No expectations. No right or wrong. Just doodle. And keep doodling. There are some blank pages here for you to express your creativity without words. Let your creativity sparkle and shine. Heck, grab the crayons and start coloring in the doodles as well!

SPARK A STORY

DEBBY JOHNSON

SPARK A STORY

DEBBY JOHNSON

SPARK A STORY

DEBBY JOHNSON

SPARK A STORY

DEBBY JOHNSON